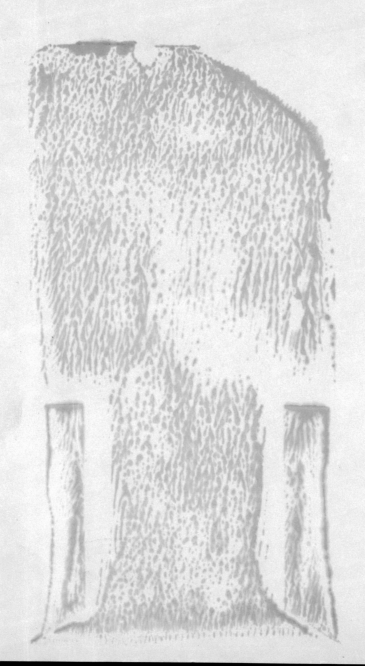

Horses

by Janusz
GRABIANSKI

FRANKLIN WATTS, INC.
845 Third Ave., New York, N. Y. 10022
SBN 531 — 01368 — 5

Everyone loves to watch a very young foal frisk and jump. He is full of life and his long legs are not steady at first, but very soon he learns to walk with smooth, springy paces.

Whatever a horse is bred for—working, racing, riding—he needs careful feeding and grooming. And he always responds to calm routine and kindness.

A working horse needs more food than other kinds of horses, in order to keep up its great strength. Draft horses like the Percheron or Ardennais must be strong and sure-footed so that they can easily pull heavy loads. Horses bringing in the hay or the harvest were at one time a common sight.

Horses do many different kinds of work.
The Quarter horse—a breed that is very
popular in the United States—is still used
to 'work' cattle and horses. A horse must
be very quick and nimble, and intelligent
to do this difficult work. Quarter horses
are also calm and willing.

You do not need a special horse for a joy-ride like this. In eastern Europe, where winters are long, there is nothing more fun than an old-fashioned sleigh jaunt on a quiet snowy evening. The sounds of the horse trotting over the snow and the jingle of the harness bells make every drive seem like Christmas-time.

A gipsy's horse has a hard life. He
pulls the family in their heavy living
wagon and has to be content with
little food, grazing where he can.
But gipsies have a loving understanding
of horses and train them well. This
man has a fine animal of Arab stock.

The Shire and the Clydesdale—British
farm horses—and the Austrian breed
called Noriker, pictured here, are all
bred for pulling tremendous weights.
In the Middle Ages it was large, muscular
horses like these that were used as
military chargers, ridden by knights.

This very heavy load is no problem at all for these draft horses in the city of Munich in southern Germany.

The pageantry of State occasions would
not be complete without horses. Here,
following the cavalry escort and mounted
police, is the traditional carriage and
four, bearing a lovely young princess
through cheering crowds.

Mules are really the most useful of
pack animals for they can carry loads
of as much as three hundred pounds
and are sure-footed on narrow,
mountainous paths and rough tracks.

This gay wagonette, or surrey, is
pulled by a handsome pet donkey.

It is rare nowadays to see horses in the midst of traffic. This handsome pair of Lipizzaners step forward proudly as the coachman flourishes his whip. Such a sight brings a breath of the past to Vienna's modern streets.

The Shetland pony is almost the
smallest horse there is. He makes a
wonderful pet, gentle and easy to ride.
Also he is an intelligent animal, who
is easy to train to perform in circuses.
It is rare to see a smaller pony than the
Shetland here, but there is a breed from
the Argentine no bigger than a
rocking-horse—the Fallabella—
which is becoming popular
in some places as a house pet.

Every kind of person turns up in the crowd at a race meeting
—fashionable and shabby, old and young—but however different
they may be, they all feel the same thrill when they hear the
starter's pistol. As the horses come galloping over the turf and
spread out at the rails a few of them pull ahead and take
the lead, but the winner at the finish may not be one of them.

Horses must have shoes
to protect their hooves.
There are still blacksmiths'
forges all over the world,
where this shoeing is done.

Schooling a horse calls for long
and patient practice, but this is
something that young people love to
do. The rider, girl or boy, sharing
with a beloved pony all the difficulties
and the triumphs of long training, comes
to know how to manage the horse in all
his moods—and learns to control his
own moods, too.

Thoroughbreds, bred specially for
racing, can gallop at a speed up to
forty miles an hour. Everything about
them suggests speed, from the long,
slender nose to the long, flowing tail.

There are various kinds of races: steeplechases over obstacles, flat races, and trotting races with horses pulling carts called 'sulkies'— as well as Show Jumping competitions. Here the Jumper is clearing the bars with apparent ease, but it has meant long and careful training to achieve this perfect, well-timed leap.

The horses used in harness racing, where the horse pulls a sulky at a quick trot, are ones specially bred for this purpose.
In America the horses used are called Standardbreds.

Fox hunting, which began in England,
has been popular for more than two hundred
years. Hunters are horses bred in England
and Ireland with this sport in view; they
arc Thoroughbreds or partly so. The rider
wears the traditional costume that
includes a red coat (called 'pink'
after the first tailor who made them—
a Mr Pyncke). There is also
'fox' hunting with an
artificially-laid trail
called drag-hunting.

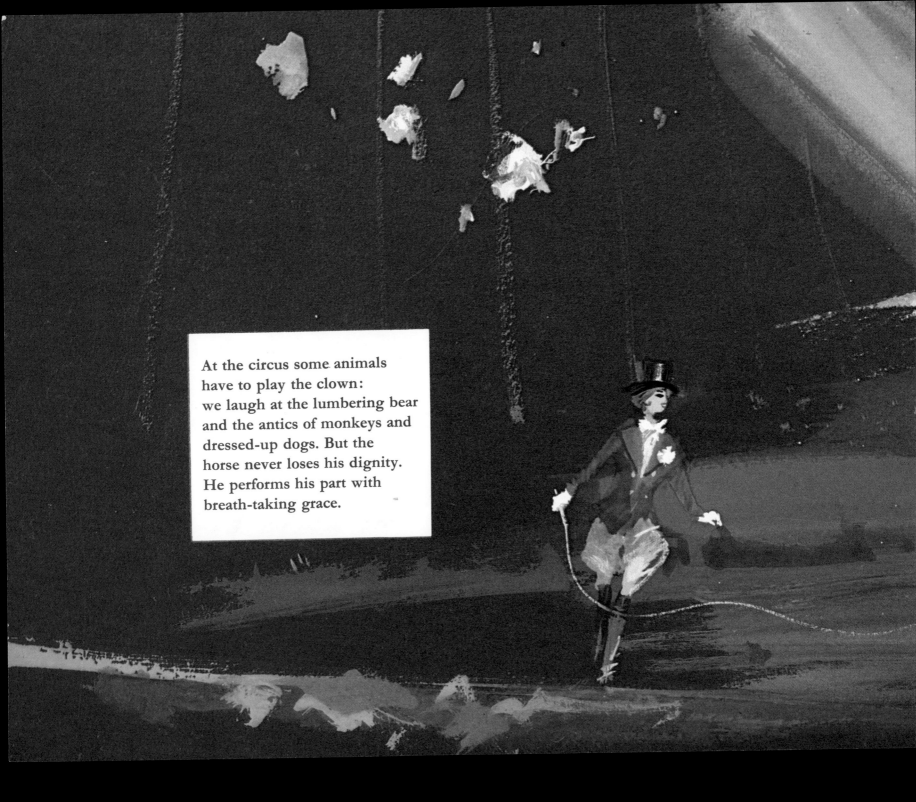

At the circus some animals
have to play the clown:
we laugh at the lumbering bear
and the antics of monkeys and
dressed-up dogs. But the
horse never loses his dignity.
He performs his part with
breath-taking grace.

This horse is a Mustang. Mustangs were wild horses directly descended from the horses that the Spanish explorers brought to America.

Polo ponies are not really a special kind of horse, just any horse that is suitable to be trained for playing polo. They must be fast, agile, and very courageous. It is the aptitude for the game that makes a good polo horse.

In Vienna is the famous Spanish Riding
School where snow-white Lipizzaner
horses are given their exacting High
School training. The two horses
here are performing the 'airs' known
as the 'levade' and the 'piaffe'.
In such performances horse and rider
seem like one being, so complete is
the harmony between them.

But the beginning is always hard.
Whether the horse is purebred or of
mixed blood, raised in stables or
roaming wild like the Australian
'brumbies', the first thing he has
to learn is to understand the wishes
of man, his master.